YELLOWSTONE

BY
Carol Marron

I wish to thank the folowing people for their help: Timothy R. Manns, North District Naturalist/Park Historian; Joe Zarki, Division of Interpretation; Roderick A. Hutchinson, Park Geologist; Anita Varley, Public Affairs Assistant, Amy Vanderbilt, Assistant Public Affairs Officer; and Don G. Despain, Research Biologist.

PUBLISHED BY
CRESTWOOD HOUSE
NEW YORK

LIBRARY OF CONGRESS CATALOGING IN PUBLICATION DATA

Marron, Carol A.
  Yellowstone

  (National parks)
  Includes index.
  SUMMARY: Describes the geography, including the geysers, hot springs, mud pots, and fumaroles, and plants and animals of Wyoming's Yellowstone Park. Includes a history of the park and a map.
  1. Yellowstone National Park — Juvenile literature. [1. Yellowstone National Park. 2. National parks and reserves.] I. Title. II. Series: National parks (Mankato, Minn.)
F722.M27   1988   978.7'52—dc19   88-18643
ISBN 0-89686-405-7

International Standard Book Number:	Library of Congress Catalog Card Number:
0-89686-405-7	88-18643

PHOTO CREDITS

Cover: Journalism Services: Harvey Moshman
Journalism Services: (Harvey Moshman) 11; (Richard Day) 27
Ned Skubic: 4, 13, 37, 39, 42-43
DRK Photo: (Don & Pat Valenti) 10; (Lewis Kemper) 15; (Stephen J. Krasemann) 16; (Tom Till) 19; (Jeff Foott) 29
Tom Stack & Associates: (Spencer Swanger) 7; (D. Jorgenson) 18; (Sharon Gerig) 20; (G.C. Kelley) 22; (Thomas Kitchin) 24-25, 32; (Diana Stratton) 30, 35; (Tom Stack) 40-41

CRESTWOOD HOUSE

Macmillan Publishing Company
866 Third Avenue
New York, NY 10022
Collier Macmillan Canada, Inc.

Printed in the United States of America
10 9 8 7 6 5 4 3 2

TABLE OF CONTENTS

Yellowstone National Park

YELLOWSTONE — LAND OF MYSTERY

In Yellowstone National Park, mud puddles boil and mountains smoke. Waterfalls tumble and dance in a canyon of gold. The earth rumbles, then shoots out steaming jets of water. Long ago, fur trappers and prospectors told eerie tales about these natural wonders. The public laughed and called them lies. Still, some settlers were curious enough to take a look for themselves.

The early explorers were excited by Yellowstone's marvels. Many felt the strange springs and geysers should be protected for future visitors. They didn't want any one person to own or destroy such rare land. The United States Congress agreed.

On March 1, 1872, President Grant signed an act removing the area from settlement. Yellowstone was set aside as a "public park or pleasuring ground." It became the first national park in all the world.

Yellowstone is a big place. Its 3,472 square miles make it larger than the states of Delaware and Rhode Island combined! Almost all of the park lies in the northwest corner of Wyoming. Narrow slivers of it spread into Idaho and Montana. This region is in the Rocky Mountain Range, an area that has

Yellowstone's marvels have fascinated visitors for many years.

5

stayed wild longer than other part of the country.

About 500 tourists traveled to Yellowstone in its first year. It was a rugged journey. Visitors had to haul their supplies over bone-jarring pony trails. Their maps were crudely drawn and the Native Americans they met were not always friendly.

Today, over two million people drive through the park each year. Many of them are families on vacation. Others are scientists who come to study this natural wonderland. These travelers have good roads and friendly rangers to help them enjoy their stay. And on cool summer nights, the geysers and springs still send up haunting clouds of fog. Then Yellowstone looks as eerie as it did 100 years ago.

OUT OF THE SEA

From the world's beginning, the earth has thrust up mountains and rain has washed them down. Again and again, earth, wind, and water have fought to shape the land. The Yellowstone region has been a battlefield in this conflict many times. Signs of the struggle can be seen in the hillsides, canyons, and riverbanks.

About 570 million years ago, broad areas of North America lay flat and low. In the west, an ancient ocean flooded parts of Yellowstone many times. The waters carried sand, plants, and sea creatures. As they died, the shells and bones of the sea animals settled with the sand. This sea debris formed layers of *sediment.*

Over millions of years, different animals lived in the sea. Some species died out, and others replaced them. In time, the oceans receded. Sediments dried and hardened into bands of sandstone, limestone, and shale. The seas left at least 25 deposits of sediment in the park.

There were no mountains in Yellowstone at that time. Water had shaped the land into a gentle, rolling plain. But powerful forces were stirring on the earth's crust. Pieces of crust called *plates* were drifting and squeezing together.

The crust of the world is like a broken egg shell. Many cool pieces of crust fit over softer and hotter rock inside. When plates bump together, rock layers slowly bend and wrinkle. If the stress becomes too great, cracks known as *faults* occur. Giant chunks of earth can push upward along such cracks. As

FUN FACT From 1920 to 1926 special permission was required to use a motion-picture camera in the park.

they slide over neighboring layers of rock, they become mountains.

Seventy-five million years ago, there was a huge disturbance in the earth's crust. The Rocky Mountain Range was driven upward by a long period of folding and faulting. At the northern part of the range, Yellowstone's beds of sediment were lifted as well.

The park's broken layers of sediment can still be seen near the Snake River banks and in the Gallatin Mountains. But most of the sediment is hidden below younger rock.

The levels of a frozen hot spring stand waiting for the spring thaw.

VOLCANO!

Under the earth's crust lies a massive layer of rock called the *mantle*. Rock in the mantle is hot and soft, like tar. If this hot rock were at the surface, it would melt by expanding and forming gas. But deep underground, it is held firm by the weight of cooler rocks above.

When the crust is broken by faulting, rock may melt and squirt upward along the faults. Molten rock is called *magma* when it is underground. At the surface it is known as *lava*.

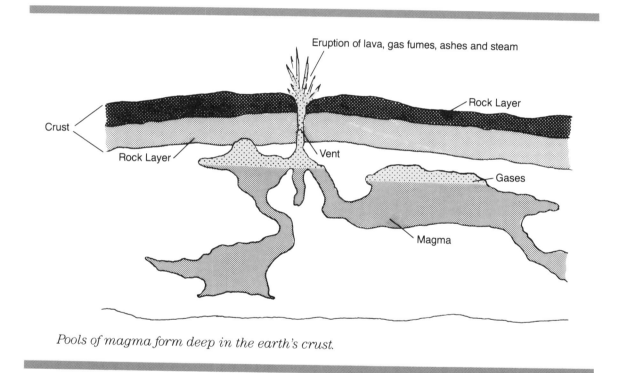

Pools of magma form deep in the earth's crust.

Pools of magma can form between layers of crust. After the Rocky Mountains were uplifted, a large chamber of magma formed under Yellowstone. This pool of magma erupted in several periods of the park's history.

Some of the first lava flows in Yellowstone built huge volcano cones. Mount Washburn and the Absaroka Range started as volcanoes. The magma that built these mountains erupted easily. Gas in the molten rock escaped with the lava.

There were often long quiet spells between the Absaroka eruptions. This happened when lava cooled in the volcano vents. In time, gas trapped in the magma below exploded. When mountains tops blew off, tons of ash and cinders swirled over the nearby forests.

The animals ran away before the deadly ash and fumes erupted, but all the plants were killed. Trees were buried in ash up to 15 feet deep. Their upper parts decayed, and the buried trunks turned to stone. Hot water seeping through the ash carried minerals into the cells of wood. The stumps were *petrified* while standing in the layer of ash.

Hundreds of years passed between these violent outbursts. Time and again, soil formed on the land's surface. New forests grew and were destroyed by further eruptions. In Specimen Ridge, near Mount Washburn, 27 petrified forests are buried one on top of another. Wind and water have exposed their stumps on the hillside. The wearing or washing away of soil and rock is called *erosion*.

Growth rings show that some of the ancient trees were 500 years old when they died. Scientists have identified redwoods, maples, oaks, and other trees that grow in warmer climates. Yellowstone was still at a lower elevation than it is today.

After a long quiet period, a huge section of the Rocky Mountains was uplifted again. Portions of Yellowstone were pulled apart into giant blocks. The Gallatin Range in the northwestern corner of the park was thrust up. Other blocks of the park sank. More volcanic action followed.

BLANKETS OF FIRE

About 600,000 years ago, the chamber of magma under Yellowstone began to rise again. It arched the ground like a giant blister. Cracks opened in the earth, reaching all the way down to the molten rock. With a sudden explosion, gas in the magma blew out through the cracks. Enormous amounts of hot dust, gas, and rock particles swept across the countryside. Old valleys and stream beds were quickly filled with burning debris.

So much magma blew out of the chamber that the ground above collapsed. A giant *crater* called a *caldera* sank several thousand feet. This "hole" was as much as 35 miles across. A smaller blister formed and collapsed in the area of Yellowstone Lake known as West Thumb.

West Thumb was formed when a "caldera" sank several thousand feet.

For thousands of years, lava oozed out of the fractures circling the calderas. *Rhyolite,* the most common type of rock in the park, came from this lava. *Obsidian* and *basalt,* two other kinds of volcanic rock, formed as well. Obsidian is the black, glassy rock the Native Americans later chipped into spear heads. Basalt is a duller black rock.

Basalt flows created some of the most interesting rock formations in Yellowstone. When basalt cools, it sometimes cracks and forms columns with five or six flat sides. There are basalt columns in Sheepeater Cliffs and along the Grand Canyon of the Yellowstone.

FUN FACT Radiator Geyser was born in one of Yellowstone's parking lots. A car was parked above it during one of its first eruptions. People nearby thought the car's radiator was boiling over!

ROTTEN EGGS OR EVIL SPIRITS?

On a frosty night, mists rising from Yellowstone form an eerie scene. Bubbles burst and plop in pools of steaming water. All around *geysers* shoot up hissing waterspouts. The ground trembles and the air smells like rotten eggs. It is easy to see why people have imagined evil spirits living here!

Some of the magma that once fueled Yellowstone's volcanoes still burns close to the ground. The chamber of molten rock may lie less than three miles deep. When water drains into cracks in the earth, it is heated by rocks near the magma. This heated water causes the thermal wonders of Yellowstone. They are often grouped together in areas called basins.

Rocks found below the earth's surface heat the basins in Yellowstone.

BLANKETS OF ICE

Grinding ice put the finishing touches on Yellowstone's landscape. During periods of cold weather, snow stayed all year on the mountains. The snow packed down into hard layers of ice called *glaciers*. The weight of the snow and ice dragged the glaciers down the mountainsides.

As the ice crept along, it crushed rock and carried the gravel with it. Sometimes glaciers blocked the flow of rivers and streams. Earth and clay settling out of the backed-up water formed broad valleys with good soil.

During the last ice age, glaciers covered most of the park. Only the western border and some of the highest mountain peaks escaped the grinding ice. When the ice finally melted, hollows in the ground filled with water and glacial lakes were formed.

GRAND CANYON OF THE YELLOWSTONE

The biggest canyon in Yellowstone is a gash in the earth over 20 miles long. At places the steep walls drop more than 1,000 feet. Although not as deep or wide as others in the country, this canyon has a beauty of its own.

The Yellowstone River rushes through the canyon, leaping over two steep ledges. Upper Falls drops 108 feet. A half-mile downstream, the water plunges 308 feet over Lower Falls. From the Lower Falls visitors can see many shades of rust and yellow rock. Almost every explorer who saw the canyon remarked on its shades of gold.

Rhyolite lava flows formed the basic rock in the canyon. For thousands of years, hot water and gases rose through sections of the stone. Slowly, the rhyolite was softened and changed to its yellow color.

Glaciers in Yellowstone did not travel through the canyon. They scraped across it and flattened the land around its rim. When the ice melted, torrents of water poured through the gorge. Gravel released by the glaciers acted like sandpaper eroding the river bed.

On a chilly morning, puffs of vapor show that steam is still forming under the canyon. Grain by grain, sand continues to be swept away with the river.

The Yellowstone River plunges down a steep ledge to form a beautiful waterfall.

Millions of years from now, the canyon will wear a new face. But the difference in one person's lifetime will hardly be noticed.

GEYSERS

Many people think geysers are the most exciting of Yellowstone's wonders. There are over 200 active geysers in the park. No other place on earth has so many geysers in one spot. In fact, there are more geysers in Yellowstone than in all the rest of the world combined!

The underground workings of a geyser.

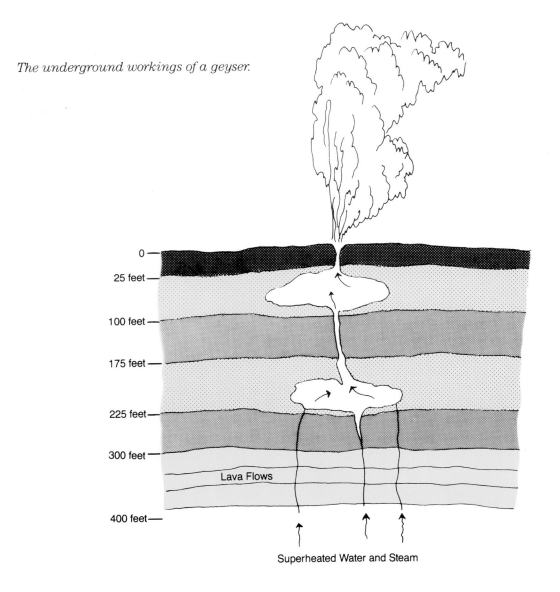

0
25 feet
100 feet
175 feet
225 feet
300 feet
Lava Flows
400 feet

Superheated Water and Steam

Riverside Geyser sprays its water at an angle; most of the other geysers shoot their water straight up.

14

What makes a geyser? To begin with, water from rain and melted snow soaks deep underground. Rock under the geyser basins allows the water to circulate near the magma chamber. Once it is heated there, it flows up and enters the geyser's plumbing system. It can take a long time for water to make this journey. Scientists say rainwater from the deepest levels may be over 400 years old!

The wells under geyser vents have narrow places that partly trap the rising water. The water is very hot, but pressure in the system keeps it from boiling at its usual temperature. Eventually, a few steam bubbles begin to form. They squirt through the tight places and push out some water sitting above.

This first splash releases the pressure on the super-heated water. Large amounts of it explode into steam, flushing out the geyser's system. The eruption lasts until steam quits forming. Then water seeps back into the plumbing system and pressure starts building again.

From time to time, a violent eruption may break the water channels in a geyser. If the water is no longer restricted, it can flow out in a constant stream. Sometimes the water leaks into other systems. No one knows when a "sleeping" geyser might start erupting again.

Old Faithful is the most famous of Yellowstone's geysers. About once every 70 minutes it spouts a column of water as high as 180 feet. The jet usually lasts from two to five minutes and reaches about 130 feet high. Park rangers time each eruption and measure the height of its spray. From these facts, they estimate when the next eruption will be. If Old Faithful erupts for a long time, it may need a longer rest period. During this break it refills and reheats the water in its system.

Not all geysers need rest periods. Some spout almost constantly. Others erupt for an hour, then sleep for days. Riverside Geyser, along the Firehole River, spouts 20 minutes every six to seven hours. Unlike most geysers that shoot straight up, Riverside sprays at an angle. Each of Yellowstone's geysers is different in size and habit. But the thermal process that causes them is all the same.

HOT SPRINGS COME IN MANY COLORS

In places where underground water can rise freely, *hot springs* form. Pools of water often collect in stone "bowls" at the spring's vent. Some, like Morning Glory Pool, reflect the blue sunlight. Sulphur Cauldron was named for the mineral that tints its water yellow. Names like "Rainbow," "Emerald," and "Lemonade" hint at the variety of colors found in many

About once every 70 minutes, Old Faithful spouts water as high as 180 feet.

The blue sunlight is reflected beautifully in Yellowstone's Morning Glory Pond.

springs.

Hot springs are often colored by tiny plants called *algae*. These microscopic organisms can live in water too hot to touch. The color of the algae shows the temperature of the pool. Green algae grows at temperatures of 120°F or less. Orange algae lives in pools of about 145°F. Yellow algae can live in water up to 160°F or so. The clear blue springs are usually too hot for algae to grow in.

Grand Prismatic is the largest hot spring in the park. It is 370 feet across. At its center, the deep water is dark blue. Algae growing at the pool's edges add rings of green, yellow, and orange. When a mist hangs over the water, these colors are reflected in the vapor, too.

Each hot spring has its own "well." The water in one may dribble out quietly. Right next door, another can be hissing and boiling. It all depends

FUN FACT Morning Glory Pool was cleaned in 1950. Over 112 different kinds of items were found in its vent. Among the debris were $86.27 in pennies; 76 handkerchiefs; socks, shirts, and underclothes.

on the plumbing system. The springs are about the same temperature both winter and summer.

As in geysers, hot water in springs can dissolve minerals in deep rock layers. Mineral deposits, called *sinter*, often accumulate around a spring's opening. Punch Bowl Spring, near the Black Sand Basin, has built up a rim of sinter. Trees near springs sometimes become encrusted with minerals and slowly petrify.

Beneath Mammoth Hot Springs, water flows through beds of limestone. Mineral deposits in this area are called *travertine*. The springs here look very different than the pools in the basins. Hot water seeping out of mountainsides leaves level "steps" of travertine. Algae growing on the hot spring terraces give delicate color to the formations.

Unlike sinter rims, travertine shelves grow and change rapidly. Water is constantly breaking through in new spots, leaving higher areas to dry out. *Geologists* estimate that two tons of minerals are deposited each day.

The largest hot spring in Yellowstone is Grand Prismatic.

MUDPOTS AND FUMAROLES

Bubbling and plopping, Yellowstone's *mudpots* look like bowls of boiling pudding. The author Rudyard Kipling thought mudpots sounded like gasps of drowning people. He didn't like them very much. "Geysers are permissible," he wrote, "but mud is terrifying."

Mudpots are hot springs with smaller supplies of water. What moisture there is mixes with acid gases. This fluid is strong enough to dissolve rock minerals. A fine clay forms and fills their vents. Sometimes rising bubbles of gas fling mud several feet high.

Mudpots are often called "paint pots." They come in a variety of colors. Their usual shades are cream, grey, and black. A few turn pink from dissolved iron. In spring, melting snow makes them thin and soupy. In late summer, the same pot may throw up thick lumps of clay.

Fumaroles are also hot springs that lack a strong water supply. In a fumarole, water is changed to steam before it reaches its vent. One of the gases that erupts with the steam is hydrogen sulfide. This gives the familiar "rotten egg" odor. Visitors may smell or hear a fumarole before they see it!

Steam and gas escaping from a noisy vent in the early 1900s gave Roaring Mountain its name. The vent roared for months, then enlarged enough for the steam to escape quietly. Fumaroles are often seen smoking on the hillsides. Visitors can hear their hissing vents throughout the park, however.

THE FIRST PEOPLE

Ancient spear tips and arrow points have been found near Yellowstone. They hint that prehistoric people wandered through the park land more than 10,000 years ago. Scientists who study the past call these people "Early Hunters." Early Hunters were always on the move. They followed the roaming mammoths and ancient bison.

After the ice ages, mammoths and other big animals disappeared. The people who lived in Yellowstone at this time were called Foragers. Foragers tended to stay in one region, moving between winter and summer camps. Season after season, small family groups returned to places where they had found food before. Roots, seeds, berries, and fish were the mainstay of their diets. Some of their simple tools have been found near Yellowstone Lake.

Some hot springs have "shelves" that grow and change rapidly.

In a quiet meadow, a bull elk calls to its herd.

About 200 years ago, tribes of Crow, Blackfeet, Bannock, and Shoshoni lived near the park land. These Native Americans probably visited the area to hunt and collect obsidian. Obsidian was prized for making tools and arrow points. Other minerals were taken for use as paint.

For 40 years, Bannock and Shoshoni tribes crossed the park on a path know as the Bannock Trail. Bison west of Yellowstone had disappeared by 1840. Rather than live without bison, these people made yearly trips east to herds in Wyoming. Whole families took the 200-mile journey.

Only one tribe of Shoshoni, the Sheepeaters, lived all year in the current boundaries of Yellowstone. Records show the Sheepeaters were a timid people. They didn't own horses or guns. Their name came from their principle source of food—the bighorn sheep.

Some Shoshonis called Yellowstone's basins "The water-that-keeps-on-coming-out." Explorers claimed the Native Americans feared the geysers and mudpots. More likely, they simply didn't have much reason to go near them. Deep snow covered the area more than half of the year. Dense forests with fallen trees made traveling difficult. Since hunting was better elsewhere, the trails near the geysers were used very little.

JOHN COLTER'S JOURNEY

Private John Colter is given credit for being the first white man to see Yellowstone. From 1803 to 1806, he was a hunter with the Lewis and Clark expedition. The purpose of this trip was to explore the Missouri River to the Pacific Ocean. On the homeward journey, Colter and the party met two American fur trappers at a Native American village. The trappers asked Colter to guide them back into the mountains. The three men spent one season together hunting beaver.

In 1807, Colter worked for a trader with the Missouri Fur Trading Company. His orders were to search the Yellowstone region for Native Americans willing to trade beaver skins. Colter traveled alone through 500 miles of uncharted Wyoming territory. The first accounts he gave of Yellowstone's wonders were either ignored or laughed at.

FUN FACT In 1903, President Theodore Roosevelt was shaving in his tent. Someone announced a herd of bighorn sheep were nearby. The President rushed out to see them with one cheek shaved and the other still lathered.

Bighorn sheep are found in the quieter sections of Yellowstone National Park.

TRAPPERS' TALES

Hunters and trappers opened the trails west for American pioneers. They gave some of the oldest English names to the country's landmarks. Bridger Lake, Sulphur Mountain, and the Gardner River are examples from the park. Mountain people played an important part in Yellowstone's discovery. But they are more often remembered for what they said than what they did.

In the early 1800s, fur companies held yearly meetings. Trappers came to trade furs, and they stayed to trade tales. One hunter might have begun by saying he'd seen a petrified tree. Another would top that by adding "petrified birds singing petrified songs"!

Over the years the stories were repeated and changed many times. A few of them suggest a setting from Yellowstone. One story describes a lake with boiling spring water on its surface. A fish caught below the hot layer could be cooked on its way out!

Stretching the truth was the trappers' way of having fun. Most of the hunters didn't care if the public believed them or not. Jim Bridger was an exception.

Bridger was one of the best guides in the frontier. He wanted his accounts of the geysers published, but editors ignored him. Jim lived to be 75 years old. That was long enough to see his reports about the geysers proven true.

THE TRUTH ABOUT WONDERLAND

During the 1860s, gold was discovered in Montana. Many times, *prospectors* trekked through Yellowstone hoping to become rich. Like the trappers, the prospectors came to use the land's resources. They weren't trying to prove the geysers and springs existed.

Very little gold was found in the park area. As the prospectors moved on to richer lands, they told tales of what they had seen. Curious settlers began to wonder if there was any truth to the rumors. The mysteries of Yellowstone were finally revealed by three parties of explorers.

In 1869, the Folsom-Cook-Peterson party spent more than a month in

FUN FACT In 1883, three men from the Laramie Bicycle Club toured the park. They rode "ordinary" bicycles. The front wheels were as tall as a car's roof and the rear was the size of tricycle's

26

As the weather gets warmer, moose and other animals find plenty to eat.

27

Yellowstone. They examined the canyon, Lake Yellowstone, and several geysers. The accounts of the three miners stirred interest in some of Montana's most important citizens.

The Yellowstone expedition of 1870 included General Henry D. Washburn. He was the surveyor general of the Montana Territory. With his authority, Old Faithful and many other features of the park were named.

After their adventure, members of the Washburn party wrote about making Yellowstone a park. Nathanial P. Langford traveled east to lecture on the value of such unusual land. One of the men who heard his speech asked Congress for money to conduct an official survey of the area.

In 1871, Ferdinand V. Hayden brought a large group of scientists to Yellowstone. A famous artist made drawings of the park, and a photographer came along to take pictures. At last, the public had proof of the geysers and springs! Congress quickly passed the act that made Yellowstone the world's first national park.

BISON AND THE U.S. CAVALRY

Some hunting was permitted in the early days of the park. Settlers took bears, squirrels, rabbits, and other small game to feed their families. *Poachers,* hunters who killed protected animals, came to Yellowstone, too. They shot and sold elk for their hides and ivory teeth. The poachers knew there were not enough park officials to stop them. They also knew wealthy people would pay hundreds of dollars for a rare bison head.

In the early 1800s, millions of buffalo, or bison, roamed the country. Trains heading west were halted by swarms of bison crossing railroad tracks. Travelers spoke of herds that spread as far as the eye could see. Fur companies and skin hunters began carelessly slaughtering the bison. Within 50 years, the bison were nearly killed off. The last wild herd was protected in Yellowstone National Park.

In 1886, the U.S. Cavalry was given control of the park. It was determined to keep the small herd of bison alive. The army captains worked hard to track down poachers. They sent small patrols into areas where animals were likely to be killed. When caught, poachers had their guns taken away. The captured men were banned from the park, but they often returned.

The Park Protection Act was passed in 1894. It gave Yellowstone's

FUN FACT   Roadside thieves were once a hazard in the park. On August 24, 1908, a single bandit held up 17 coaches and wagons. His loot was $1,365.95 in cash and $730.25 in watches and jewelry.

officials power to fine and jail poachers. These stricter measures finally stopped most of the killing. However, serious damage to the bison herd had already been done. By the early 1900s, fewer than 100 bison were counted in the park.

In 1902, Congress gave Yellowstone $15,000 to buy bison from private collectors. A man known as "Buffalo Jones" helped deliver three males from Texas, and 15 females from Montana. As gamekeeper, Jones cared for these animals in a corral at Mammoth Hot Springs. Five years later the bison were moved to a larger fenced area in the Lamar Valley. The herd grew and the

A small elk family searches for food in one of the park's streambeds.

Today, about 3,000 bison live in Yellowstone National Park.

animals were gradually released. They joined the few remaining free bison and took on their wild habits.

Bison in Yellowstone now number close to 3,000 animals. Visitors see them most easily in winter when they graze along the road between Mammoth Hot Springs and the Lamar Valley. In the summer they go to the high country to escape biting flies.

Saving the bison is one of the success stories of Yellowstone Park!

FUN FACT Cars were not allowed in the park until 1915. That year a Model "T" Ford was the first official tourist car to enter Yellowstone.

"GOOD ANIMALS AND BAD ANIMALS"

Every time pioneers settled into a wilderness area, they began to change it. *Predators*, animals who kill and eat other animals, were often trapped or poisoned. Wolves, cougars, and coyotes were considered "bad" animals because they ate the game people wanted for themselves.

In Yellowstone, park officials worried that predators would harm the herds of elk and deer. In the early days, army commanders directed their men to kill wolves and coyotes. By the 1930s, in fact, thousands of coyotes had been killed.

Because the numbers of elk were increasing, park managers thought they were doing the right thing. But hungry elk began to eat more than their share of twigs, leaves, and grass. Herds of deer, antelope, and bighorn sheep dwindled.

Eventually studies showed that lack of winter food, not predators, was the cause of the decrease in game animals. Park management began taking a new direction. They no longer tried to make changes in the park's wildlife. Nature, it was decided, knew how to take care of itself.

Changes in the numbers of Yellowstone's animals and plants are now seen as parts of long natural cycles. When left alone, the species find a balance for themselves. This system is called natural regulation.

TRUMPETER SWANS

Along the riverbank, a pair of trumpeter swans are building their nest. The female works steadily. She is eager to have her nursery finished. The male stops often to preen his brilliant white feathers. Looking up, he spots an intruder and calls out a warning.

The invading trumpeter is full grown. His wingspan is nearly ten feet across. The nesting pair must defend their territory. Together they pull his tail feathers and nip his wings. The trespasser soon retreats. Then the mates put on a joyous triumph display. Facing one another, they stretch their trembling wings and trumpet their victory.

A black bear cub finds safety in a high tree branch.

About 12 pairs of majestic trumpeter swans nest in the park's lakes and rivers. Because hot springs keep many areas free from ice, some of these swans stay all year. Years ago, open water from Yellowstone's hot springs helped save the trumpeter swan from *extinction*.

After the demand for beaver pelts dried up, some fur companies began selling swan skins. The Hudson's Bay Company sold over 17,000 skins during the 1800s. Individual hunters killed many more during the fall migrations. The swan's feathers were stuffed into quilts and blankets. The skins and down were made into powder puffs.

By 1932 there were only 69 swans in the United States. They were found just west of Yellowstone, in an area where hot springs kept the lakes from freezing. If they had migrated from this remote spot, hunters would probably have killed them, too.

In 1935, the federal government set aside Red Rock Lakes, Montana, as a migratory bird refuge. The number of swans there has gradually increased. More trumpeters have been discovered in Canada and Alaska. All of these birds are protected by strict laws.

Every year, hundreds of trumpeters come to spend winter in the park. The swans do not defend their territories in this season. They flock peacefully near Yellowstone's lakes and rivers.

NO "TEDDY BEARS"!

Many tourists who visit Yellowstone hope to see a bear. About 500 black bears and 200 grizzlies roam through the park. Although black bears are not as ferocious as grizzlies, they have caused injuries. Begging bears seem tame, but their interest is only in getting something to eat. A bear feels no regret if a piece of finger is taken along with a bite of cookie.

In nature, bears and humans do not mix well. They compete for the same land and food supply. Native Americans and fur trappers steered clear of bears. They knew a surprised grizzly, especially a worried mother, could be a deadly foe. Luckily, bears prefer to avoid people, too.

In Yellowstone, the early tourists were more interested in the geysers than in the bears. But the bears were very interested in the garbage tourists left behind. Like people, bears are *omnivorous*. This means they eat both plants and animals. Bears are not very fussy. A piece of spoiled chicken or rotting

FUN FACT Female bears guard their cubs from male bears who often eat them. Mother bears may be quick to attack people because they think humans are as dangerous as male bears.

fruit tastes just fine. Scraps stolen from campsites and garbage dumps were easy and tasty meals.

By the turn of the century, "bear watching" in the garbage dumps became a popular activity. Beginning in 1919, park rangers even gave nature talks while bears feasted nearby. People and bears began to lose their respect for each other's space. The numbers of injuries and property damage began to increase. Bear programs at the dumps were stopped in 1941, but bears continued to feed there. They also used more dangerous ways of getting free meals.

Although it was against the rules, visitors fed "beggar bears" along the park roadways. Generations of cubs learned that people gave handouts. Some bears became bold enough to steal into campsites at night. All too often, these bears repeated their looting and had to be shot.

Eventually park staff began strictly enforcing the rules against feeding the bears. The last open garbage dump was closed in 1972. At first rubbish was collected daily and burned in large incinerators. Now it is hauled out of the park in bear-proof trucks.

Not everyone was happy about the changes. Some people worried that hungry bears would become a bigger problem in the campground. It did take a few years for bears to adjust to their new situation. But the numbers of injuries and amounts of property damage are now much lower.

In 1975, the grizzly bear was declared a threatened animal under the Endangered Species Act. Most of Yellowstone is prime grizzly habitat. Time and the efforts of people who care about bears will determine if the grizzly survives in Yellowstone. In the meantime, any bear seen in the park is a wild bear. It is eating and roaming the way bears have done for hundreds of years.

THINGS THAT GROW

Many edible plants and flowers grow in Yellowstone. Nodding onions, fireweed, whitebark pine nuts, and bitterroot were part of the Native American diet. Today, only the animals are allowed to "pick" the flowers. Grizzlies are fond of the yampa and spring beauty. Ducks and geese eat water buttercups. Moose prefer the flowers of the sticky geranium, while deer and elk find the mountain dandelions tasty.

On a July morning, the meadows on Mount Washburn are especially

FUN FACT There were as many as 100 bear injuries a year when hotel dumps were open. Injuries are now closer to one or two a year. In some years there are none at all!

Yellowstone is home to many black bears.

good places to see Yellowstone's wildflowers. But flowers can be found almost everywhere—even on the rocky soil of the geyser basins. Heat from the thermal features allows the yellow monkeyflower to live all year long. In spring it sends up blooms several weeks before most other flowers appear. Another plant found near the geysers is the rocky mountain blue fringed gentian. This is the official Yellowstone Park Flower.

The most common trees in the park are the lodgepole pines. They shade almost two-thirds of the park's ground. Some lodgepoles grow so close together that direct sunlight doesn't reach the lower parts of their trunks. Then needles and cones are only produced at the tops of the trees. The lower branches die and fall off.

Yellowstone's vegetation zones range from cold desert to *alpine* tundra. The park has a small sagebrush desert growing near Gardiner, Montana. It includes greasewood, saltbush, and pricklypear. In the mountains, arctic plants thrive above 10,000 feet. At this height, roundleaf and snow willows grow no more than an inch high.

Aspen, douglas-fir, subalpine fir, and whitebark pine are a few of the other trees found in the park. Field guides and pamphlets are available at Yellowstone's visitor centers. These guides describe the hundreds of plants and flowers that live in the region.

VISITING THE PARK

Each year over two million tourists pass through one of Yellowstone's five entrances. Some will spend only a day rushing from one attraction to another. Even this short stay offers some unforgettable views. However, many guests are so enchanted by the scenery they decide to extend their visits.

There are lots of things to do in Yellowstone. Naturalists give guided walks through many areas. Evening programs are scheduled at the visitor centers. More than 1,000 miles of trails are open for overnight and day hiking.

Fishing with artificial lures and flys is allowed at most locations in the park. The rules for fishing, however, are made with animals in mind. Pelicans, bears, and other creatures depend on Yellowstone's fish to survive. Anglers need to learn the rules and get a free permit before fishing. Lucky guests are encouraged to throw back any fish they catch.

FUN FACT The first president to visit the park was Chester A. Arthur in 1883. A full troop of cavalry escorted his party. Men were stationed every 20 miles to provide communication with the outside world.

Lodgepole pines shade many areas in Yellowstone.

Fishing trips and boat rides are available on Yellowstone Lake. Old West cookouts, trail rides, and stagecoach rides are organized at Roosevelt Lodge. Horseback riding is also offered at Canyon and Mammoth Hot Springs. Visitors can take guided bus tours from the lodges.

Each season in the park has its own charm. In the spring waterfalls are swollen with water from melting snow. Summer brings a spectacular display of wild flowers. In autumn the trees dress up in sparkling reds and golds. Winter brings the elk and bison down to feed near the steaming hot springs. Whatever time of year they arrive, visitors experience nature at its best in Yellowstone National Park.

CHANGE

The Act that made Yellowstone a park had two requirements. The first was to provide pleasure for the park's human visitors. The second was to protect its wildlife and natural wonders. At times these two orders seem to oppose one another. Bears and hikers would like to use the same trails. Fishing fans and pelicans would like to catch the same fish.

Park managers try hard to satisfy their two goals. But changes made to suit tourists will almost always disrupt nature in some way. Grant Village, the newest hotel complex, was built near grizzly fishing streams. To balance this loss, park officials are closing facilities near other bear trails.

Destructive tourists have ruined some of the park's treasures. Handkerchief Pool was destroyed when someone jammed it with logs. Objects thrown into Thud Geyser included pop bottles, tin cans, and a frying pan. Chip by chip, one of the park's petrified trees was completely stolen by souvenir hunters.

A close-up look at one of Yellowstone's waterfalls is a special treat.

In every season of the year, Yellowstone shows off its beauty.

At times nature itself has altered the park's features. One night in 1959 a severe earthquake jolted the park. Hundreds of geysers erupted at once! Many of the geysers went through drastic changes in their cycles. In 1983, another big quake made Old Faithful's eruptions hard to predict for several months.

FUN FACT The first speed limits in the park were: 10 miles per hour (m.p.h.) going down a hill, 12 m.p.h. going up a hill, and 8 m.p.h. when approaching a curve.

Although some changes have occurred and others cannot be avoided, Yellowstone is still a land of wonder. For the most part, the animals that mountain people observed still roam the forest and meadows. The geysers and mudpots still put on their amazing performances. And curious people still come to see if what they've been told is true.

FUN FACT The water in Sulphur Cauldron and a few other springs is as acid as the fluid in a car battery.

Although Yellowstone National Park has gone through some changes, it is still a land of wonder and beauty.

FOR MORE PARK INFORMATION

For more information about Yellowstone National Park, write to:

National Park Service Interior
Box 168
Yellowstone National Park, WY 82190

PARK MAP

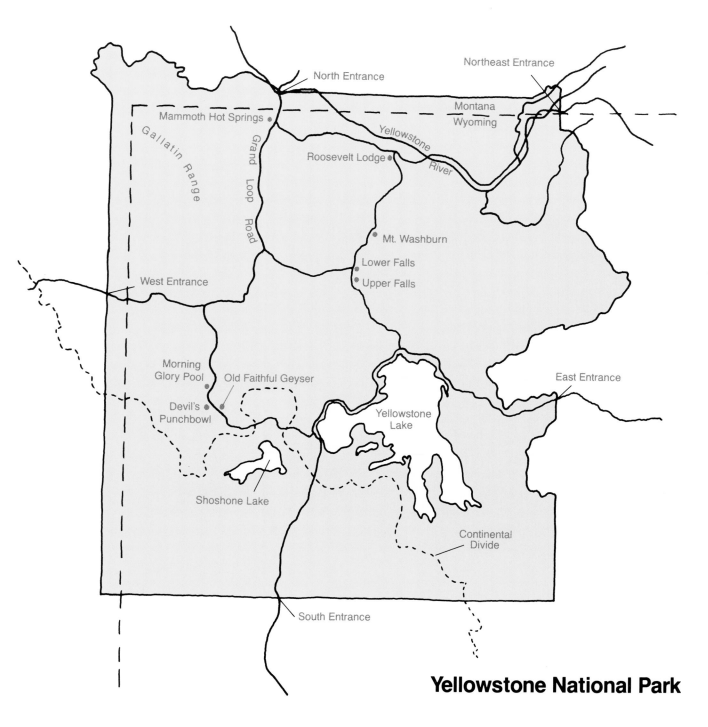

North Entrance

Northeast Entrance

Mammoth Hot Springs

Montana
Wyoming

Gallatin Range

Grand Loop Road

Yellowstone River

Roosevelt Lodge

Mt. Washburn

Lower Falls

Upper Falls

West Entrance

Morning Glory Pool

Old Faithful Geyser

Devil's Punchbowl

East Entrance

Yellowstone Lake

Shoshone Lake

Continental Divide

South Entrance

Yellowstone National Park

GLOSSARY/INDEX

ALGAE *17, 19*—Tiny water plants that live in water.

ALPINE *36*—Referring to high mountains.

BASALT *10*—A dark-colored rock formed by lava. It sometimes cools into columns with five or six flat sides.

CALDERA *9, 10*—A large crater that is formed by the collapse of a volcanic eruption.

CRATER *9*—A bowl or basin at the opening of a volcano.

EROSION *9, 12*—The washing or wearing away of soil and rock.

EXTINCTION *33*—The loss of an animal, as when the last member of a species dies.

FAULTS *6, 7, 8*—Cracks in the earth's surface.

FUMAROLES *21*—Openings in the ground where steam and gas are released. Fumaroles are the dry form of a hot spring.

GEOLOGIST *19*—A person who studies the history of the earth and how its changes are recorded—especially in rocks and rock formations.

GEYSER *5, 11, 14, 15, 17, 19, 21, 23, 26, 28, 33, 36, 38, 40, 41*—A spring that throws a column of water and steam into the air.

GLACIERS *12*—Masses of ice formed from hard-packed snow that remain frozen a long time.

HOT SPRINGS *17, 18, 19, 21, 28, 29, 30, 33, 38*—An opening in the ground containing water heated in rock layers below.

LAVA *8, 9, 10, 12*—Melted rock flowing from a break in the earth's crust.

MAGMA *8, 9, 11, 15*—Melted rock below the earth's surface.

MANTLE *8*—The hot layer of rock between the earth's surface and its core.

MUDPOTS *21, 23, 41*—A hot spring with a small water supply that forms mud at its vent.

OBSIDIAN *10, 23*—A dark, glassy rock that forms when lava cools and hardens quickly.

OMNIVOROUS *33*—An animal that eats both plants and animals.

PETRIFY *9*—To turn to stone from mineral deposits.

PLATES *6*—Huge slabs of the earth's crust that slowly drift about.

POACHER *28*—One who kills game illegally.

PREDATORS *31*—Animals that kill or eat other animals.

PROSPECTOR *5, 26*—One who examines a region for gold or other valuable minerals or ores.

RHYOLITE *10, 12*—Volcanic rock with high silica content.

SEDIMENT *6, 7*—Particles of sand and other materials that settle to the bottom of rivers, lakes, and oceans.

SINTER *19*—Mineral deposits of silica that are formed by hot springs and geysers.

TRAVERTINE *19*—A form of limestone deposited by hot springs.